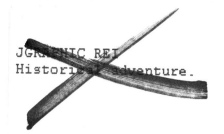

JGRAPHIC REI
Historical adventure.

A Connecticut Yankee in King Arthur's Court

AS ON A VISIT TO WARWICK CASTLE THAT
ET HENRY MORGAN, A CURIOUS OLD FELLOW
O KNEW EVERYTHING THERE WAS TO KNOW
UT ARMS AND ARMOR.

AROUND THE WORLD IN 80 DAYS

DAILY STANDARD

From London to Suez via Brindisi, by rail and steamboats: 7 days
From Suez to Bombay, by steamer:13 days
From Bombay to Calcutta, by rail: 3 days
From Calcutta to Hong Kong, by steamer: 13 days
From Hong Kong to Yokohama, by steamer: 13 days
From Yokohama to San Francisco, Japan, b...
From San Francisco to San Francis...
From New Yor...

TOTA...

The Prisoner of ZENDA

Please visit our Web site at: www.garethstevens.com
For a free color catalog describing World Almanac® Library's
list of high-quality books and multimedia programs,
call 1-800-848-2928 (USA) or 1-800-387-3178 (Canada).
World Almanac® Library's fax: (414) 332-3567.

Library of Congress Cataloging-in-Publication Data available upon request from publisher.
Fax (414) 336-0157 for the attention of the Publishing Records Department.

ISBN-13: 978-0-8368-7927-8 (lib. bdg.)
ISBN-13: 978-0-8368-7934-6 (softcover)

This North American edition first published in 2007 by
World Almanac® Library
A Member of the WRC Media Family of Companies
330 West Olive Street, Suite 100
Milwaukee, Wisconsin 53212 USA

"A Connecticut Yankee in King Arthur's Court" adapted by Henry Barker, illustrated by Dan Spiegle from *A Connecticut Yankee in King Arthur's Court* by Mark Twain. Copyright © 1999 by Bank Street College of Education. Created in collaboration with *Boys' Life* magazine. First published in *Boys' Life* magazine, December 1999, by the Boy Scouts of America. Reprinted by permission of Bank Street College of Education and *Boys' Life* magazine.

"Around the World in 80 Days" adapted by Shannon Lowry, illustrated by Dan Spiegle, lettering and color by Tom Luth from *Around the World in 80 Days* by Jules Verne. Copyright © 2007 by Bank Street College of Education. Created in collaboration with *Boys' Life* magazine. First published by World Almanac® Library, 2007. Printed by permission of Bank Street College of Education and *Boys' Life* magazine.

"The Prisoner of Zenda" adapted by Henry Barker and E. A. M. Jakab, illustrated by Dan Spiegle from *The Prisoner of Zenda* by Anthony Hope. Copyright © 1999 by Bank Street College of Education. Created in collaboration with *Boys' Life* magazine. First published in *Boys' Life* magazine, October 1999, by the Boy Scouts of America. Reprinted by permission of Bank Street College of Education and *Boys' Life* magazine.

This U.S. edition copyright © 2007 by World Almanac® Library.

World Almanac® Library editorial direction: Mark Sachner
World Almanac® Library editors: Monica Rausch and Tea Benduhn
World Almanac® Library art direction: Tammy West
World Almanac® Library designer: Scott Krall
World Almanac® Library production: Jessica Yanke and Robert Kraus

Printed in Canada

1 2 3 4 5 6 7 8 9 10 10 09 08 07 06

A Connecticut Yankee in King Arthur's Court

ON A VISIT TO WARWICK CASTLE THAT HENRY MORGAN, A CURIOUS OLD FELLOW NEW EVERYTHING THERE WAS TO KNOW ARMS AND ARMOR.

A Connecticut Yankee in King Arthur's Court

IT WAS ON A VISIT TO WARWICK CASTLE THAT I MET HENRY MORGAN, A CURIOUS OLD FELLOW WHO KNEW EVERYTHING THERE WAS TO KNOW ABOUT ARMS AND ARMOR.

By Mark Twain

Adapted By Henry Barker

Illustrations By Dan Spiegle

HENRY AND I TOOK SUPPER TOGETHER, AND SAT TALKING FAR INTO THE NIGHT. BEFORE RETIRING, HENRY GAVE ME THE MOST ASTONISHING DOCUMENT I HAVE EVER READ. IT WAS AN ACCOUNT OF HIS LIFE.

IT HAS BEEN A PLEASURE, MR. TWAIN. FORGIVE ME, BUT I GROW WEARY. SINCE YOU ARE A WRITER OF FANCIFUL TALES, YOU MIGHT FIND MY OLD JOURNAL INTERESTING.

THE PLEASURE IS MINE, MR. MORGAN. I SHALL GO HOME RIGHT NOW AND READ IT! SLEEP WELL.

BRIDGEPORT, CONNECTICUT?

CAMELOT.

AS WE CAME INTO THE COURTYARD, A PAGE NAMED CLARENCE ANSWERED SOME OF THE QUESTIONS WHIRLING IN MY HEAD. HE SEEMED SANE ENOUGH— IN SPITE OF WHAT HE TOLD ME.

NOW TELL ME, HONEST AND TRUE, WHAT YEAR IS THIS AND WHERE AM I?

THE YEAR IS 528—JUNE 19 TO BE EXACT—AND YOU ARE IN KING ARTHUR'S COURT.

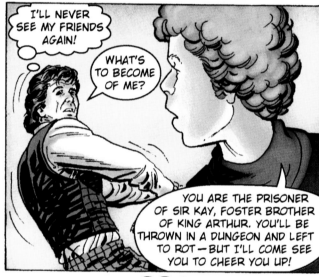

I'LL NEVER SEE MY FRIENDS AGAIN!

WHAT'S TO BECOME OF ME?

YOU ARE THE PRISONER OF SIR KAY, FOSTER BROTHER OF KING ARTHUR. YOU'LL BE THROWN IN A DUNGEON AND LEFT TO ROT—BUT I'LL COME SEE YOU TO CHEER YOU UP!

YOU WILL BE BURNED AT THE STAKE IN TWO DAYS! AND MERLIN, THE MAGICIAN, HAS CAST A SPELL ON YOU SO NO ONE WILL SAVE YOU.

TELL THE KING I'M A MAGICIAN—A MUCH GREATER ONE THAN MERLIN. IF HE DARES HARM ME, I WILL SMOTHER THE WORLD IN BLACKNESS—ALL THE PEOPLE SHALL DIE.

WHY HASN'T THE ECLIPSE STARTED? HAVE I MADE A MISTAKE IN MY CALCULATIONS?

BUT THEN THE SKY BEGAN TO DARKEN.

STRANGER! NAME ANY TERMS, EVEN HALF MY KINGDOM! ONLY END THIS HORROR!

NOW YOU SEE THE POWER OF MY MAGIC. THE DARKNESS WILL END AT MY COMMAND.

BY THE TIME THE ECLIPSE WAS OVER, CAMELOT WAS IN THE PALM OF MY HAND.

I BEGAN ADVISING THE KING ON MATTERS OF STATE. I WAS A YANKEE AND DIDN'T BELIEVE IN FANCY TITLES SO I REFUSED THE KING'S OFFER TO MAKE ME A DUKE OR AN EARL. I PREFERRED SOMETHING SIMPLER. FROM THAT TIME ON, I WAS KNOWN AS "THE BOSS."

I CHALLENGE YOU TO PERFORM ANOTHER MIRACLE!

HAPPY TO OBLIGE.

EXCELLENT ADVICE, SIR BOSS!

THANK YOU, SIRE.

IN TWO WEEKS TIME, I WILL PERFORM ONE FINAL MIRACLE— I WILL BLOW UP MERLIN'S TOWER. I CHALLENGE MERLIN TO STOP ME!

WITH CLARENCE'S HELP, I MADE SOME FIRST-RATE BLASTING POWDER AND PLACED IT IN THE TOWER WALLS. WE CROWNED THE TOWER WITH A LIGHTNING ROD AND RAN WIRES FROM THE ROD TO THE POWDER. THEN ALL WE HAD TO DO WAS WAIT FOR LIGHTNING TO STRIKE.

KA-BOOM!

BY MY LIFE! THOU ART TRULY A MAGICIAN WITHOUT EQUAL!

IT WAS NOTHING, SIRE.

NOTHING?!

MERLIN LEARNED HIS LESSON—FOR A WHILE. HE STAYED OUT OF MY HAIR FOR THE NEXT FOUR YEARS, WHICH WAS FORTUNATE BECAUSE I HAD A LOT TO DO. THE COUNTRY NEEDED MODERNIZING. I SET UP A SCHOOL SYSTEM..

...AND STARTED A NEWSPAPER...

DRAWBRIDGE COLLAPSES! KNIGHTS BATTLE RUST!

...AND I FOUNDED SEVERAL FACTORIES AND SECRETLY LAID WIRES FOR A TELEPHONE AND TELEGRAPH NETWORK.

HELLO? CAN YOU HEAR ME, CLARENCE?

AS IF YOU WERE IN THE NEXT TURRET!

I WAS MAKING REAL PROGRESS, UNTIL...

...THE LADY ALISANDE CAME TO CAMELOT. THREE OGRES HAD IMPRISONED HER MISTRESS AND 44 OTHER PRINCESSES IN THEIR CASTLE. THE LADIES NEEDED RESCUING.

PRITHEE, YOUR MAJESTY, APPOINT ONE OF THY GOODLY KNIGHTS TO RESCUE MY MISTRESS!

SIR BOSS! HERE'S AN ADVENTURE FOR YOU!

RATS!

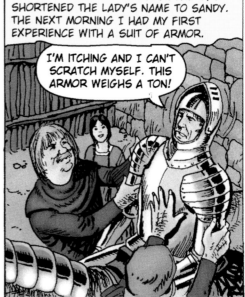

THE KING SUGGESTED I TAKE LADY ALISANDE WITH ME, SINCE SHE KNEW WHERE THE PRINCESSES HAD BEEN TAKEN. TO MAKE THINGS MORE MANAGEABLE, I SHORTENED THE LADY'S NAME TO SANDY. THE NEXT MORNING I HAD MY FIRST EXPERIENCE WITH A SUIT OF ARMOR.

I'M ITCHING AND I CAN'T SCRATCH MYSELF. THIS ARMOR WEIGHS A TON!

IT ONLY GOT WORSE. I WAS HOT AS BLAZES INSIDE MY ARMOR, AND HUNGRY BESIDES. THREE HOURS OUT ON MY FIRST ADVENTURE, AND I WAS FED UP WITH CHIVALRY.

AREN'T THE FLOWERS LOVELY, MY LORD?

SANDY, HOW CAN THEY CALL THIS A SUIT? IT DOESN'T HAVE ANY POCKETS! A MAN CAN'T EVEN CARRY A SANDWICH FOR HIS LUNCH.

BUT I FORGOT MY TROUBLES. A GROUP OF "FREE MEN" PAUSED IN THEIR LABOR TO SHARE THEIR FOOD WITH US. THEY TOLD ME ABOUT THEIR LIVES.

YOU SAY THAT THREE DAYS OUT OF SEVEN YOU MUST WORK UNPAID FOR YOUR MASTER?

AYE.

AND YOU OWE YOUR MASTER PART OF THE PROCEEDS WHEN YOU SELL YOUR LAND?

AYE, AND ALSO WHEN WE BUY IT.

AND YOU CAN'T GROW WHEAT, OR GRIND IT, OR EVEN BAKE BREAD WITHOUT PAYING YOUR MASTER FOR THE PRIVILEGE?

AYE.

THESE AREN'T FREE MEN. THEY'RE SLAVES!

I RESOLVED TO TURN ENGLAND INTO A REPUBLIC, SO THAT ALL HER PEOPLE—NOT JUST THE NOBILITY—WOULD BE FREE. THEN I REMINDED MYSELF THAT I WAS IN THE SIXTH CENTURY, NOT THE 19TH, AND KEPT MY MOUTH SHUT. MY PLANS WOULD STAY SECRET FOR NOW.

THERE IS THE CASTLE!

CASTLE? IT'S NOTHING BUT A PIGSTY, SANDY!

IT IS UNDER AN ENCHANTMENT!

SANDY, BEING AS SUPERSTITIOUS AS MOST PEOPLE OF THIS ERA, BELIEVED THE PIGS WERE ENCHANTED LADIES, AND I FOUND IT EASIER TO GO ALONG WITH HER.

MY LADY! YOUR HIGHNESS! YOUR GRACE! YOU ARE NO LONGER IN PERIL. MY BRAVE KNIGHT HAS RESCUED THEE!

I'LL TAKE ALL OF THEM.

THIS IS AN ADVENTURE, ALL RIGHT.

AFTER THE RESCUE OF THE PIGS —ER, PRINCESSES—WE FELL IN WITH SOME PILGRIMS BOUND FOR THE VALLEY OF HOLINESS. IN THE VALLEY WAS A MONASTERY WHOSE FOUNTAIN BOASTED HEALING POWERS. AS WE APPROACHED...

THE HOLY FOUNTAIN HAS DRIED UP! BECAUSE YOU COULD NOT BE FOUND, SIR BOSS, MERLIN WAS SENT FOR. HE SAYS ONLY HIS POWERFUL MAGIC CAN REPAIR THE FOUNTAIN.

WE'LL SEE ABOUT *THAT!*

KNIGHT, TAKE A MESSAGE TO CAMELOT FOR ME!

OF COURSE, SIR BOSS!

Clarence:
I need two packets of No. 3 and six packets of No. 4 from the chemical department, a water pump and an electrical kit pronto! Send them to the Valley of Holiness with two assistants.
The Boss

WITH SOME HELP FROM CLARENCE, I KNEW I COULD WORK A SPECTACULAR MIRACLE. I JUST HAD TO STALL FOR A FEW DAYS SO THE BOYS COULD GET HERE WITH SUPPLIES.

DON'T LET ME INTERRUPT YOU, OLD BOY.

#!!&*!!@

IT DIDN'T EVEN OCCUR TO MERLIN TO EXAMINE THE WELL.

IT IS A DIFFICULT MIRACLE TO RESTORE A DRIED-UP WELL, BUT I WILL TRY. ONCE MY ESTEEMED BROTHER MERLIN HAS MADE HIS ATTEMPT.

THAT SHOULD BUY ME SOME TIME!

JUST AS I SUSPECTED. A SIMPLE LEAK!

MERLIN HAD NO LUCK WITH HIS POTIONS AND SPELLS. AS SOON AS MY ASSISTANTS ARRIVED FROM CAMELOT, WE SET TO WORK.

GOOD TO SEE YOU, BOYS!

THERE! THE LEAK'S REPAIRED.

THE PUMP'S INSTALLED.

AND THE FIREWORKS ARE READY. BOYS, THIS IS GOING TO BE ONE HUMDINGER OF A MIRACLE!

THE BOYS AND I WAITED FOR THE SUSPENSE TO BUILD.

THEN I GAVE THE SIGNAL...THE "MAGIC WORD" THAT WOULD START THE MIRACLE.

CONSTANINOPALITANISCHERDUDELSACH-SPFIEFENMACHERSGESELLLSCHAFT!

ARTHUR TRIED, BUT HE MADE A TERRIBLE COMMONER. WHILE TRYING TO POSE AS A FARMER WITH SOME LOCAL TOWNSFOLK, HE ONLY CONVINCED EVERYONE HE WAS CRAZY.

SOME SAY THE ONION IS POISONOUS WHEN PICKED TOO EARLY FROM THE TREE, BUT IN MY OPINION, PLUMS AND OTHER CEREALS SHOULD ALWAYS BE DUG UP UNRIPE...

GOD HATH SURELY SMITTEN THE MIND OF THIS FARMER!

...INDEED, THEY ARE AT THEIR MOST WHOLESOME THIS WAY, ESPECIALLY WHEN MIXED WITH THE JUICE OF THE WILD CABBAGE...

SIRE! I MEAN FARMER JONES! IT GROWS LATE...IT IS TIME FOR US TO GO...

...UNLIKE THE GOAT, WHICH RIPENS QUICKLY AND SOON BECOMES RANCID!

HE'S STARK RAVING MAD!

MAD, AM I? WHY, YOU...

THE TOWNSFOLK TURNED ON US, DRIVING US UP A TREE AND THEN SETTING IT ON FIRE.

THE SMOKE WAS OVERWHELMING. WE FINALLY GAVE OURSELVES UP.

AS THE MOB SEIZED US, A NOBLEMAN, EARL GRIP, AND HIS RETINUE APPEARED.

UNHAND THESE MEN!

EARL GRIP INVITED US TO JOIN HIS PARTY, ASSURING US WE WOULD BE SAFE WITH HIM.

WAIT UNTIL I TELL HIM WHO WE ARE! HE'LL BE RICHLY REWARDED FOR HIS KINDNESS; I'LL SEE TO THAT.

BUT WHEN WE GOT TO THE NEXT TOWN...

WHO ARE THESE POOR WRETCHES?

SLAVES.

SLAVES?

SHACKLE THEM!

THIS IS AN OUTRAGE! I AM THE KING!

SURE YOU ARE! AND I AM JULIUS CAESAR!

WE WERE SOLD AT AUCTION LIKE SWINE AND FORCE-MARCHED TO LONDON.

I FOUND A WAY TO ESCAPE THAT TERRIBLE LONDON CELL.

BY A STROKE OF LUCK I FOUND ONE OF OUR SECRET TELEPHONE OFFICES.

SEND LANCELOT WITH 500 KNIGHTS TO LONDON! THE KING IS IN PRISON! HE'S BEEN ENSLAVED!

RIGHT AWAY, SIR BOSS!

I LEARNED THAT OUR OWNER HAD FLOWN INTO A RAGE OVER MY ESCAPE. HE BEAT THE OTHER SLAVES SO VICIOUSLY THAT THEY FOUGHT BACK...AND KILLED HIM. NOW WE WERE ALL CONDEMNED TO DIE.

YOU'LL ALL HANG FOR THIS!

MY HEART SANK AS TWO, THEN THREE SLAVES WERE PUT TO DEATH.

I FEAR IT'S TOO LATE FOR ANYONE TO SAVE US!

THAT NOISE! IT SOUNDS LIKE...

...BICYCLES!

WHAT STRANGE STEEDS ARE THESE? PRAY, TELL ME, LANCELOT!

WHEN I LANDED IN ENGLAND, I COULD HARDLY BELIEVE MY EYES AND EARS.

WHAT AM I BID FOR THIS FINE-LOOKING FELLOW? HE'S ONLY 14 AND STRONG AS AN OX!

WHAT HAS HAPPENED SINCE I'VE BEEN AWAY? THIS IS A NIGHTMARE!

I HASTENED TO CAMELOT. IT WAS DARK AND DESERTED.

ONLY ONE DIM LIGHT IN ALL OF CAMELOT. HOW STRANGE!

SIR BOSS! YOU'VE COME BACK!

SUPERSTITION, JEALOUSY AND HATRED HAD SWEPT THROUGH THE COUNTRY LIKE A PLAGUE, DIVIDING THE KING AND HIS COURT. SOME KNIGHTS HAD SIDED WITH SIR LANCELOT; OTHERS WITH KING ARTHUR. A TERRIBLE BATTLE HAD LAIN THEM ALL TO WASTE.

KING ARTHUR IS DEAD. LANCELOT TOO. AND ALL THE BEST KNIGHTS OF THE ROUND TABLE.

NOW THEY WERE GONE, ALONG WITH ALL SIGNS OF PROGRESS—AND MY DREAM OF A REPUBLIC.

SIR BOSS, I HAVE TRAINED A GROUP IN SECRET. LIKE YOU, THEY DREAM OF FREEDOM. IF YOU LEAD, THEY WILL FOLLOW.

WE'LL FIGHT TO THE DEATH FOR FREEDOM FROM TYRANNY, SIR BOSS!

THE NEXT MORNING WE CALLED THE TOWNSFOLK TOGETHER, AND ISSUED A PROCLAMATION.

WHEREAS THE KING HAS DIED AND LEFT NO HEIR, THE MONARCHY NO LONGER EXISTS. ALL MEN ARE EXACTLY EQUAL AND A REPUBLIC IS HEREBY PROCLAIMED.

A REPUBLIC? I'M FOR IT!

SO AM I!

LONG LIVE THE REPUBLIC!

LONG LIVE THE BOSS!

I FEARED THE COUNTRY MIGHT TURN AGAINST US, AND IT DID. A WEEK LATER, THE ATTACK BEGAN. THERE WERE 54 OF US, AND ABOUT 30,000 OF THEM...BUT WE WERE READY.

HERE GOES!

OH NO! THE EXPLOSIONS WE SET OFF ARE GOING TO TRAP US INSIDE THIS CAVE!

A FEW DAYS LATER...

WE CAN'T GET OUT. DISEASE...FROM ALL THE DEAD AND WOUNDED... IT'S KILLING US ALL!

I, CLARENCE THE PAGE, HAVE TAKEN OVER SIR BOSS' JOURNAL BECAUSE HE FELL ILL AND LOST CONSCIOUSNESS. JUST NOW, I NOTICED AN OLD CRONE CROUCHED OVER HIM. TOO LATE, I REALIZED WHO SHE WAS!

MERLIN! GET AWAY FROM SIR BOSS! WHAT ARE YOU DOING?

YOU SHALL ALL DIE IN THIS PLACE — EXCEPT HIM! HE'LL WAKE IN 1,300 YEARS!

the Boss does not stir. If any of us ever escapes from here, that survivor has promised to hide this manuscript with the Boss, our dear good chief and friend.
Clarence the Page

I MUST GO TO HENRY IMMEDIATELY! WHAT AN INCREDIBLE STORY.

I RUSHED INTO HENRY MORGAN'S ROOM TO FIND MY FRIEND CLOSE TO DEATH. HENRY WAS UTTERING HIS LAST WORDS...

SANDY! HELLO OPERATOR! OH, I'VE MISSED YOU SO!

THE END

MARK TWAIN, OR SAMUEL L. CLEMENS

"MARK TWAIN" IS THE PEN NAME OF SAMUEL LANGHORNE CLEMENS, AN AMERICAN WRITER KNOWN FOR HIS SHARP WIT AND SATIRE. CLEMENS WAS BORN IN FLORIDA, MISSOURI, ON NOVEMBER 30, 1835, AND MOVED WITH HIS FAMILY TO HANNIBAL, MISSOURI, WHEN HE WAS FOUR YEARS OLD. HIS YEARS GROWING UP IN THIS TOWN ALONG THE MISSISSIPPI RIVER WOULD INFLUENCE HIS LATER WORKS. AS A TEENAGER HE WORKED AS A PRINTER'S APPRENTICE AND, LATER, TRAVELED AND FOUND A JOB AS A PRINTER. IN 1857, HE BEGAN WORKING AS A MISSISSIPPI RIVER BOAT PILOT, A TOUGH AND DANGEROUS JOB THAT REQUIRED NAVIGATING THE CHANGING CURRENTS AND SANDBARS OF THE MISSISSIPPI. HE WORKED UNTIL 1861, WHEN THE CIVIL WAR PUT AN END TO MUCH NON-MILITARY SHIPPING ON THE RIVER. THIS JOB, HOWEVER, GAVE HIM THE IDEA FOR HIS PEN NAME. "MARK TWAIN" IS CALLED OUT BY A SHIP'S CREW MEMBER WHEN THE WATER IS TWO FATHOMS, OR ABOUT 4 YARDS (3.7 METERS), DEEP AND SAFE FOR TRAVEL. IN 1862, HE STARTED TRAVELING THROUGHOUT THE UNITED STATES AND WRITING AS A NEWSPAPER JOURNALIST. HIS FIRST BOOK, **THE INNOCENTS ABROAD** (1869), IS A COLLECTION OF HUMOROUS LETTERS ABOUT HIS TRAVELS THAT HE HAD WRITTEN TO NEWSPAPERS. HE WROTE SHORT STORIES, AND NOVELS SOON FOLLOWED, INCLUDING **THE ADVENTURES OF TOM SAWYER** AND **THE ADVENTURES OF HUCKLEBERRY FINN**. HE PUBLISHED **A CONNECTICUT YANKEE IN KING ARTHUR'S COURT** IN 1889. CLEMENS EXPERIENCED MUCH TRAGEDY IN HIS LIFE, LOSING THREE OF HIS FOUR CHILDREN AND HIS WIFE, OLIVIA LANGDON, DURING HIS LIFETIME. HE ALSO HAD HAD HARD TIMES FINANCIALLY, ALTHOUGH HE WAS AN EXTREMELY POPULAR AND WELL-KNOWN WRITER BEFORE HIS DEATH IN 1910.

A Connecticut Yankee in King Arthur's Court!

...AS ON A VISIT TO WARWICK CASTLE THAT
...T HENRY MORGAN, A CURIOUS OLD FELLOW
...KNEW EVERYTHING THERE WAS TO KNOW
...UT ARMS AND ARMOR.

AROUND THE WORLD IN 80 DAYS

DAILY STANDARD

From London to Suez via Brindisi, by rail and steamboats: 7 days
From Suez to Bombay, by steamer:13 days
From Bombay to Calcutta, by rail: 3 days
From Calcutta to Hong Kong, by steamer: 13 days
From Hong Kong to Yokohama, by steamer: 13 days
From Yokohama to San Francisco, Japan, by steamer: 6...
From San Francisco to New York...
From New York to London...

TOTAL: 80 DA...

The Prisoner of ZENDA

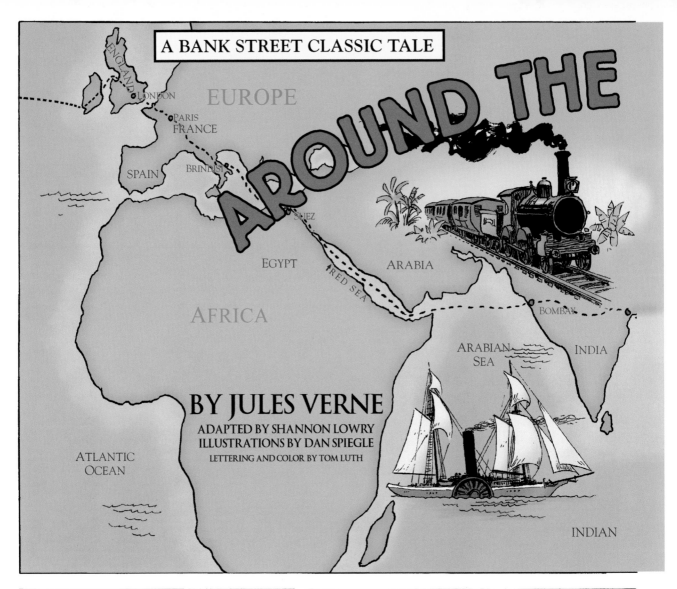

A BANK STREET CLASSIC TALE

AROUND THE

BY JULES VERNE

ADAPTED BY SHANNON LOWRY
ILLUSTRATIONS BY DAN SPIEGLE
LETTERING AND COLOR BY TOM LUTH

JEAN PASSEPARTOUT--FORMER PARISIAN CIRCUS PERFORMER, STREET MUSICIAN, GYMNASTICS COACH AND FIREMAN--CRAVED A QUIETER LIFE. IN THE FALL OF 1872, HE APPLIED TO WORK FOR THE QUIETEST, MOST ORDERLY MAN IN ENGLAND. LITTLE DID HE KNOW THE EXCITEMENT AND ADVENTURE THAT LAY AHEAD!

MY WATCH SAYS IT IS 11:22 A.M., MR. FOGG.

YOUR WATCH IS FOUR MINUTES SLOW. FROM THIS MOMENT, 11:26 A.M., OCT. 2, 1872, YOU ARE IN MY SERVICE.

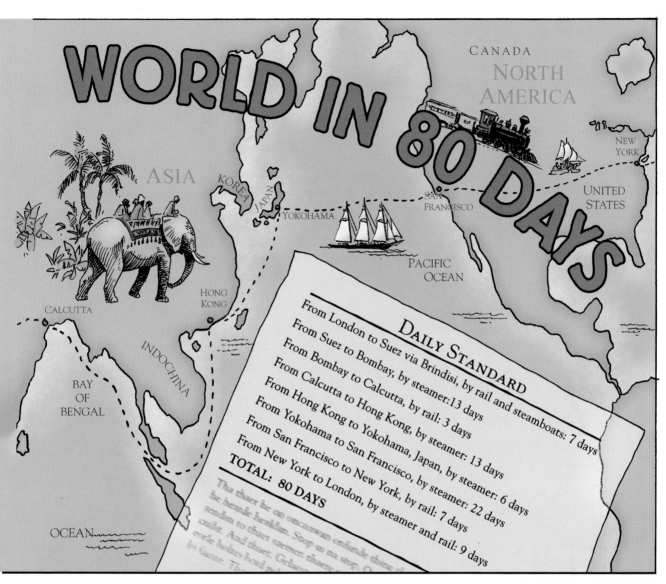

WORLD IN 80 DAYS

CANADA
NORTH AMERICA

ASIA

KOREA
JAPAN
YOKOHAMA

NEW YORK

UNITED STATES

SAN FRANCISCO

PACIFIC OCEAN

CALCUTTA

HONG KONG

INDOCHINA

BAY OF BENGAL

OCEAN

DAILY STANDARD

From London to Suez via Brindisi, by rail and steamboats: 7 days

From Suez to Bombay, by steamer:13 days

From Bombay to Calcutta, by rail: 3 days

From Calcutta to Hong Kong, by steamer: 13 days

From Hong Kong to Yokohama, Japan, by steamer: 6 days

From Yokohama to San Francisco, by steamer: 22 days

From San Francisco to New York, by rail: 7 days

From New York to London, by steamer and rail: 9 days

TOTAL: 80 DAYS

THEN PHILEAS FOGG LEFT WITHOUT ANOTHER WORD.

I'VE SEEN FIGURES AT THE WAX MUSEUM LIVELIER THAN MY NEW MASTER!

IN HIS ROOM, PASSEPARTOUT FOUND A LIST OF HIS CHORES ON THE MANTEL.

WE SHALL GET ALONG WELL! MR. FOGG STICKS TO THE SAME ROUTINE EVERY DAY!

FOGG WALKED EXACTLY 575 STEPS TO THE REFORM CLUB FOR A LATE BREAKFAST...

READ THE PAPERS UNTIL 5:10 P. M.,

AND ATE DINNER AT 5:20 P.M.

AT EXACTLY 6:10 P.M., FOGG WAS JOINED FOR A GAME OF WHIST BY HIS USUAL PARTNERS. ONE OF THEM, GAUTHIER, WAS A DIRECTOR OF THE BANK OF ENGLAND.

GAUTHIER, WHAT CAN YOU TELL US ABOUT THE 55,000 POUNDS JUST STOLEN FROM THE BANK OF ENGLAND?

THE BANK HAS OFFERED A HUGE REWARD FOR THE THIEF'S CAPTURE.

THEY'LL NEVER CATCH HIM. THE WORLD IS BIG ENOUGH TO HIDE HIM.

HOGWASH! THE WORLD HAS GROWN SMALLER. A MAN CAN QUICKLY CIRCLE IT NOW. THAT'S WHY WE WILL CATCH HIM.

DO YOU THINK THE WORLD IS SMALLER JUST BECAUSE YOU CAN GO AROUND THE GLOBE IN THREE MONTHS?

I'D LIKE TO SEE YOU DO IT IN 80 DAYS! I'LL BET 4,000 POUNDS IT IS IMPOSSIBLE.

SO WILL EACH OF US!

IN 80 DAYS, TO BE EXACT.

I'D LIKE NOTHING BETTER THAN TO DO IT. AND I WILL BEGIN AT ONCE.

I WILL TAKE THE 8:45 TRAIN FROM LONDON TONIGHT.

TODAY IS WEDNESDAY, OCT. 2. I WILL RETURN ON SATURDAY, DEC. 21, AT 8:45 P.M., OR ELSE THIS CHECK FOR 20,000 POUNDS IS YOURS.

THAT IS 1,920 HOURS OR 115,200 MINUTES FROM THE TIME THE TRAIN LEAVES.

ACCORDING TO YOUR SCHEDULE, YOU'RE NOT DUE HOME UNTIL MIDNIGHT!

WE'RE TAKING A TRAIN IN 10 MINUTES TO GO AROUND THE WORLD IN 80 DAYS.

PACK A CARPETBAG WITH TWO CHANGES OF CLOTHING. WE'LL BUY OTHER CLOTHES ON THE WAY.

SURELY HE IS JOKING! AROUND THE WORLD? I WANTED A QUIET LIFE!

THIS BOOK HAS THE SCHEDULES OF STEAMERS AND RAILWAYS AROUND THE GLOBE. AND HERE'S 20,000 POUNDS TO PUT IN THE CARPETBAG. TAKE GOOD CARE OF IT.

I CERTAINLY WILL, SIR!

AT THE STATION, FOGG PURCHASED TWO TICKETS TO THE PORT OF DOVER, WHERE THEY WOULD TAKE A BOAT ACROSS THE CHANNEL TO FRANCE, THEN TAKE THE TRAIN TO PARIS.

HERE, MY GOOD WOMAN. I WON THIS MONEY AT CARDS TONIGHT.

BLESS YOU, SIR!

WHAT A KIND GENTLEMAN MR. FOGG IS!

TRACK 5

I WILL HAVE EACH PORT OF CALL STAMP MY PASSPORT SO YOU CAN SEE HOW I ACCOMPLISHED MY JOURNEY. IN 80 DAYS, WE WILL MEET AGAIN. GOODBYE!

GOODBYE!

A WEEK AFTER FOGG'S DEPARTURE, A TELEGRAM ARRIVED AT SCOTLAND YARD IN LONDON.

TELEGRAM

P. FOGG IS BANK ROBBER STOP SEND ARREST WARRANT TO BOMBAY ASAP STOP DETECTIVE FIX

NEWS OF THE TELEGRAM SPREAD QUICKLY.

FOGG'S DESCRIPTION DOES MATCH THAT OF THE ROBBER!

HE TOOK OUR BET TO GO AROUND THE WORLD TO THROW DETECTIVES OFF HIS TRACK!

MEANWHILE, FOGG AND PASSEPARTOUT REACHED PARIS.

LONDON
PARIS
BRINDISI

WE HAVE 10 MINUTES TO REACH THE TRAIN STATION.

IT'S GOOD TO SEE PARIS AGAIN!

THEY HOPPED A TRAIN TO TURIN, ITALY, THEN TO BRINDISI, REACHING THIS PORT ON OCT. 5.

ON OCT. 6, THEY SAILED ON THE STEAMER MONGOLIA, HEADING FOR BOMBAY, INDIA, THROUGH THE SUEZ CANAL.

IMAGINE GOING AROUND THE WORLD AND NOT WISHING TO SEE ANYTHING!

ALL MR. FOGG DOES IS EAT, READ AND PLAY WHIST!

DETECTIVE FIX WAS ON THE SUEZ DOCK WHEN THE MONGOLIA STOPPED TO TAKE ON COAL.

I'LL HAVE MY PASSPORT STAMPED HERE BY THE BRITISH CONSUL.

I'LL BUY US SOME NEW CLOTHES.

THAT MAN FITS THE THIEF'S DESCRIPTION! THAT MUST BE FOGG!

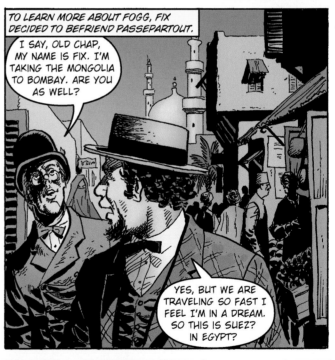

TO LEARN MORE ABOUT FOGG, FIX DECIDED TO BEFRIEND PASSEPARTOUT.

I SAY, OLD CHAP, MY NAME IS FIX. I'M TAKING THE MONGOLIA TO BOMBAY. ARE YOU AS WELL?

YES, BUT WE ARE TRAVELING SO FAST I FEEL I'M IN A DREAM. SO THIS IS SUEZ? IN EGYPT?

YES, IN EGYPT. WHICH IS IN NORTH AFRICA. YOU MUST BE IN A GREAT HURRY IF YOU ARE NOT SURE WHERE YOU ARE.

I'M NOT IN A HURRY, BUT MY MASTER IS. I MUST BUY US CLOTHES FOR THIS WARM WEATHER.

THERE'S A GOOD SHOP.

MY MASTER IS GOING AROUND THE WORLD IN 80 DAYS. HE SAYS IT IS ON A BET. HE EVEN OFFERED THE MONGOLIA'S CAPTAIN A REWARD TO GET US TO BOMBAY AHEAD OF SCHEDULE.

AH! WHAT A CHARACTER MR. FOGG IS!

PASSEPARTOUT RETURNED TO THE SHIP, BUT FIX STOPPED AT THE TELEGRAPH OFFICE FIRST.

I WILL WIRE SCOTLAND YARD, THEN FOLLOW FOGG TO BOMBAY, WHERE MY WARRANT WILL BE WAITING AND I CAN ARREST HIM.

WE ARE MAKING INCREDIBLE SPEED. YOU'D THINK WE WERE IN A RACE TO GET TO BOMBAY.

THE SHIP WAS FULL OF BRITISH OFFICERS RETURNING TO INDIA AND COUPLES ON VACATION. BUT THE JOYFUL SCENE WAS LOST ON FOGG, WHO PLAYED WHIST IN SILENCE.

FOGG HASN'T MOVED IN FIVE HOURS. YOU COULD SET YOUR WATCH BY THE MAN'S HABITS!

AT NOON ON OCT. 20, THEY REACHED BOMBAY A FULL TWO DAYS AHEAD OF SCHEDULE. PASSEPARTOUT, MEET ME AT THE TRAIN STATION AT 8 P.M. I'M GOING TO THE CONSUL TO HAVE MY PASSPORT STAMPED.

IN THE OLD DAYS, TRAVEL FROM BOMBAY TO CALCUTTA WAS BY HORSEBACK, ON FOOT OR BY CARRIAGE, AND TOOK MANY WEEKS. IN THE 19TH CENTURY, WHEN INDIA BECAME PART OF THE BRITISH EMPIRE, THE TRIP TOOK ONLY THREE DAYS THANKS TO THE NEWLY BUILT RAILWAY.

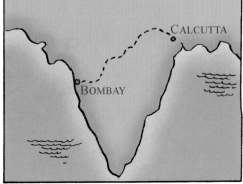

CALCUTTA

BOMBAY

FIX LEFT THE SHIP AND WENT TO THE TELEGRAPH OFFICE.

ARE YOU SURE THERE IS NO WARRANT? IT SHOULD HAVE COME DAYS AGO!

I AM SORRY, SAHIB. NO TELEGRAM FOR YOU.

TELEGRAPH

MEANWHILE, PASSEPARTOUT, CAUGHT UP IN A RELIGIOUS CARNIVAL, STEPPED INTO A LOCAL PLACE OF WORSHIP.

BLASPHEMY! YOU CANNOT COME IN HERE WITH SHOES ON! AFTER HIM!

GET OUT! GET OUT! YOU HAVE BROKEN OUR RELIGIOUS LAWS!

I DIDN'T KNOW. I'M SORRY! WHOA! I'VE GOT TO GET OUT OF HERE!

PASSEPARTOUT RUSHED INTO THE STATION AT 5 MINUTES TO 8. HE EXPLAINED HIS MISFORTUNE IN A FEW BREATHLESS WORDS.

I HOPE THIS WILL NOT HAPPEN AGAIN.

I PROMISE IT WON'T, MR. FOGG.

HMMM... FOGG'S SERVANT COMMITTED A CRIME. I'LL HAVE THEM BOTH ARRESTED IN CALCUTTA!

ON THE TRAIN WAS SIR FRANCIS CROMARTY, A GENERAL ON HIS WAY TO JOIN BRITISH TROOPS AT BENARES.

YOUR SERVANT ENTERED A PAGODA WITH HIS SHOES ON. HAD HE BEEN CAUGHT, THE BRITISH GOVERNMENT HERE WOULD PUNISH HIM.

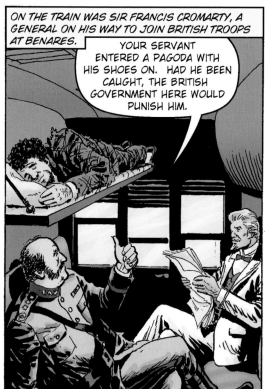

THE TRAIN STOPPED SUDDENLY IN THE COUNTRYSIDE.

THE RAILWAY ISN'T FINISHED. ALL PASSENGERS MUST GET OFF AND FIND THEIR OWN WAY TO ALLAHABAD, WHERE THE TRACKS TO CALCUTTA PICK UP AGAIN.

OUTRAGEOUS! FROM HERE TO ALLAHABAD IS 50 MILES!

PASSEPARTOUT, SEARCH THE VILLAGE FOR ANOTHER MEANS OF TRANSPORTATION.

FORTUNATELY, I AM TWO DAYS AHEAD OF SCHEDULE. THE STEAMER LEAVES CALCUTTA FOR HONG KONG AT NOON ON OCT. 25. THIS IS THE 22ND. WE CAN MAKE IT.

THIS MAN WILL SELL US HIS ELEPHANT, KIOUNI, AND I'VE HIRED A PARSEE GUIDE TO LEAD US.

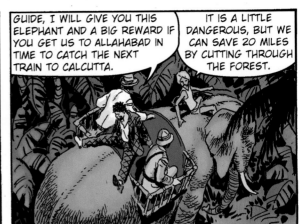

GUIDE, I WILL GIVE YOU THIS ELEPHANT AND A BIG REWARD IF YOU GET US TO ALLAHABAD IN TIME TO CATCH THE NEXT TRAIN TO CALCUTTA.

IT IS A LITTLE DANGEROUS, BUT WE CAN SAVE 20 MILES BY CUTTING THROUGH THE FOREST.

THE PARTY CAMPED OVERNIGHT IN A CLEARING ONLY 12 MILES FROM ALLAHABAD.

WHAT A MAGNIFICENT ANIMAL!

SHHHHH! SOMEONE IS COMING! WE MUST HIDE!

IT'S A SUTTEE! A LONG OUTLAWED PRACTICE. THE WOMAN IS TO BE BURNED TOMORROW AT DAWN WITH HER DEAD HUSBAND, THE POWERFUL RAJAH OF THIS REGION. SHE TRIED TO ESCAPE, BUT HIS RELATIVES CAPTURED HER. THEY WANT TO INHERIT BOTH HIS FORTUNE AND HERS.

I HAVE 12 HOURS TO SPARE. LET US SAVE HER!

WHY, MR. FOGG, YOU ARE A MAN OF HEART!

THEY FOLLOWED THE PROCESSION AND WAITED FOR THE GUARDS TO FALL ASLEEP.

THOSE GUARDS AREN'T SLEEPY.

A CHANCE MAY PRESENT ITSELF AT THE LAST MOMENT.

HMMM I HAVE A PLAN.

DAWN CAME BUT THERE WAS STILL NO OPPORTUNITY TO SAVE THE WOMAN.

THERE'S NOTHING YOU CAN DO. YOU'LL BE KILLED, TOO.

LET ME GO!

THE JUDGE SENTENCED BOTH PASSEPARTOUT AND FOGG TO JAIL OR A FINE.

I'LL PAY OUR FINES, YOUR HONOR.

YOU ARE FREE TO GO.

THE RASCAL! I'LL BRING HIM TO JUSTICE IF I HAVE TO FOLLOW HIM TO THE ENDS OF THE EARTH! BUT I STILL HAVEN'T RECEIVED THAT WARRANT!

THEY CAUGHT THE RANGOON TO HONG KONG. SO DID FIX.

RANGOON

I MUST STOP FOGG AT HONG KONG! IT'S THE LAST BRITISH TERRITORY HE WILL VISIT. I'LL WIRE THE POLICE WHEN WE STOP IN SINGAPORE.

ON OCT. 30, ONLY ONE DAY FROM SINGAPORE, FIX DECIDED TO TALK TO PASSEPARTOUT.

WHY, MR. FIX, WE LEFT YOU IN BOMBAY AND HERE YOU ARE BOUND FOR HONG KONG!

I'VE BEEN SEASICK SO I HAVEN'T BEEN ON DECK. HOW IS MR. FOGG? HOW IS HIS TIMETABLE? IS HE STILL PLAYING WHIST?

FIX ASKED SO MANY QUESTIONS ABOUT FOGG, PASSEPARTOUT WONDERED IF HE HAD BEEN SENT BY THE REFORM CLUB TO SPY ON HIS MASTER.

MR. FOGG WOULD BE HURT IF HE KNEW. I WON'T TELL HIM.

ARE YOU GOING ALL THE WAY AROUND THE WORLD WITH US?

AS USUAL, FOGG KEPT TO HIS ROUTINE.

I'M VERY FOND OF MR. FOGG. BUT WHILE HE IS KIND TO ME IN EVERY WAY, HE HARDLY NOTICES ME.

IT'S JUST HIS WAY. HE'S VERY METHODICAL.

DUE TO A STORM, THE RANGOON REACHED HONG KONG 24 HOURS BEHIND SCHEDULE. LUCKILY, THE CARNATIC, THE STEAMER TO YOKOHAMA, WAS STILL IN PORT FOR REPAIRS AND WOULD LEAVE THE NEXT DAY. HOWEVER, FOGG'S SEARCH FOR AOUDA'S UNCLE WAS FRUITLESS.

I'LL GO BOOK THREE CABINS FOR US ON THE CARNATIC.

YOUR UNCLE MOVED TO HOLLAND TWO YEARS AGO. YOU MUST GO ON TO EUROPE WITH US.

WHY, I DON'T KNOW. PERHAPS.

I DO NOT WISH TO INTRUDE.

PASSEPARTOUT RAN INTO FIX AT THE STEAMER OFFICE. FIX'S ARREST WARRANT HAD STILL NOT ARRIVED.

SO YOU HAVE DECIDED TO GO ON WITH US TO AMERICA?

UNFORTUNATELY YES.

THE CARNATIC'S BOILER IS FIXED. SHE WILL LEAVE AT SEVEN TONIGHT, NOT TOMORROW.

FIX DECIDED TO ASK PASSEPARTOUT'S HELP IN CAPTURING FOGG.

THE BANK OF ENGLAND WAS ROBBED OF 55,000 POUNDS. FOGG IS THE THIEF. HELP ME KEEP HIM IN HONG KONG UNTIL I GET AN ARREST WARRANT AND WE WILL SPLIT THE REWARD.

NEVER! MR. FOGG IS NOT A ROBBER AND I WON'T BETRAY HIM!

WHACK

OOF!

WAITER, THIS MAN WAS CAUSING TROUBLE. PUT HIM ON A COT IN THE BACK AND LET HIM GO WHEN HE WAKES UP.

AT THE DOCK THE NEXT MORNING, FOGG AND AOUDA RAN INTO FIX.

I SAY, OLD CHAP, DID YOU ALSO MISS THE CARNATIC? SHE SAILED LAST NIGHT WITHOUT NOTICE. THERE WON'T BE ANOTHER STEAMER TO YOKOHAMA FOR A WEEK.

I WONDER IF PASSEPARTOUT SOMEHOW WENT ABOARD THE CARNATIC AND SAILED WITHOUT US?

NOTHING TO BE DONE ABOUT IT FOR NOW. COME ALONG, AOUDA. WE MUST FIND ANOTHER SHIP.

FOGG MADE A DEAL WITH JOHN BUNSBY, CAPTAIN OF THE TANKADERE, 45 MINUTES LATER.

IT'LL BE TOUGH BUT I'LL TRY TO GET YOU TO JAPAN BY THE 14TH SO YOU CAN CATCH THE BOAT TO SAN FRANCISCO.

GOOD. MR. FIX, YOU'RE WELCOME TO ACCOMPANY US.

ER, HOW GENEROUS OF YOU.

THE 800-MILE VOYAGE WAS PERILOUS. AT THIS TIME OF YEAR, THE CHINA SEA IS SUBJECT TO TERRIBLE GALES. SURE ENOUGH, A TYPHOON CAME UP THE NIGHT OF NOV. 8.

I THINK WE SHOULD MAKE FOR ONE OF THE PORTS ON THE COAST, TO SHANGHAI.

AS THE TANKADERE SAILED INTO THE SHANGHAI PORT, AN AMERICAN STEAMER BOUND FOR YOKOHAMA WAS HEADING OUT.

SIGNAL THE SHIP! SOUND YOUR CANNON.

BOOM!

THE AMERICAN STEAMER STOPPED. FOGG, AOUDA AND FIX WERE TAKEN ABOARD AND WERE SOON ON THEIR WAY.

THEY REACHED YOKOHAMA ON NOV. 14. FOGG HURRIED TO THE CREW OF THE CARNATIC TO ASK IF PASSEPARTOUT HAD ARRIVED ON THAT SHIP THE DAY BEFORE.

YES, HE WAS ABOARD. I HEAR HE'S JOINED A LOCAL CIRCUS GROUP TO EARN HIS PASSAGE TO AMERICA.

AOUDA AND FOGG SEARCHED ALL DAY AND WERE ABOUT TO GIVE UP WHEN THEY SPIED A THEATER GROUP CALLED THE LONG NOSES FORMED INTO A HUMAN PYRAMID. AS THEY WALKED UP, THE PYRAMID COLLAPSED.

AH, MY MASTER!

HUH?

WHOA!

WHAT ARE YOU DOING?

AHHHHHH!!!

YOU IDIOT!

PASSEPARTOUT? COME ALONG. WE'RE ABOUT TO CATCH THE STEAMER GENERAL GRANT TO SAN FRANCISCO.

NOT WISHING TO UPSET FOGG BY TELLING HIM OF FIX'S ACCUSATION, PASSEPARTOUT SAID HE HAD FAINTED AFTER HITTING HIS HEAD. HE HAD NOT SEEN FIX COME ABOARD THE STEAMER AND ASSUMED HE HAD BEEN LEFT BEHIND.

I CAME TO ONLY IN TIME TO STUMBLE ABOARD THE CARNATIC AND THEN I FAINTED AGAIN. WHEN I WOKE, I REALIZED YOU TWO WERE NOT ON BOARD.

NEVER MIND. HERE IS SOME MONEY. GO TO THE SHIP'S STORE AND BUY CLOTHES THAT ARE MORE FITTING.

FIX SECRETLY HAD BEEN ABOARD THE GENERAL GRANT. HE HAD RECEIVED HIS ARREST WARRANT IN YOKOHAMA, AND DECIDED TO TRAIL FOGG ACROSS AMERICA TO LONDON.

MY WARRANT IS NO GOOD HERE IN SAN FRANCISCO, BUT IT WILL BE IN ENGLAND. I MUST TALK TO PASSEPARTOUT.

AOUDA AND I WILL GO HAVE MY PASSPORT STAMPED. PASSEPARTOUT, YOU GO BUY TRAIN TICKETS TO NEW YORK.

PASSEPARTOUT WAS NOT PLEASED TO SEE THE DETECTIVE.

O.K., I DESERVED THAT. I'M SORRY. BUT FROM NOW ON, I WON'T PUT ANY OBSTACLES IN MR. FOGG'S WAY.

SO YOU ARE CONVINCED HE IS AN HONEST MAN?

NO, I THINK HE'S A THIEF. BUT I WILL HELP HIM REACH LONDON QUICKLY IF YOU PROMISE NOT TO TELL HIM WHO I AM.

ALL RIGHT. BUT AT THE LEAST SIGN OF TREACHERY, I'LL WRING YOUR NECK!

FOGG HAD NEITHER GAINED NOR LOST A DAY REACHING SAN FRANCISCO. NOW THE PARTY WAS HURTLING ACROSS THE AMERICAN WEST ON A TRAIN THAT WOULD REACH NEW YORK IN SEVEN DAYS.

MAY I JOIN YOU? I'VE BEEN CALLED BACK TO LONDON UNEXPECTEDLY BY MY COMPANY.

MR. FIX, WHAT A PLEASANT SURPRISE.

AS THEY NEARED OMAHA, NEBRASKA, INDIANS SUDDENLY ATTACKED THE TRAIN.

THE ENGINEER IS WOUNDED. WE MUST STOP THE TRAIN BEFORE IT PASSES THE FORT FIVE MILES FROM HERE OR THE SOLDIERS WON'T BE ABLE TO COME TO OUR HELP!

I'LL STOP THE TRAIN!

THE SKILLS OF A CIRCUS PERFORMER CAN SOMETIMES BE OF USE!

PASSEPARTOUT STOPPED THE TRAIN IN TIME AND THE SOLDIERS CAME QUICKLY. BUT THE INDIANS HAD ALREADY RIDDEN OFF WITH THREE HOSTAGES.

THE INDIANS HAVE TAKEN PASSEPARTOUT!

I'LL GET HIM BACK. FIX, STAY HERE WITH AOUDA. IF ANYTHING HAPPENS TO ME...

OF COURSE, I'LL TAKE CARE OF HER.

THE TRAIN WAS BEHIND SCHEDULE AND HAD TO LEAVE WITHOUT THEM. AOUDA STOOD WATCH OUTSIDE IN THE COLD ALL NIGHT. AT DAWN, THE POSSE RETURNED WITH THE HOSTAGES.

THEY ARE SAFE!

ER, I MET A MAN NAMED MUDGE LAST NIGHT WHO HAS A SLEDGE THAT SAILS ACROSS THE SNOW. WE CAN TAKE IT TO OMAHA TO CATCH THE NEXT TRAIN TO NEW YORK.

BY THE TIME THEY SETTLED INTO THE SLEDGE FOR THE FAST, COLD RIDE TO OMAHA, FOGG WAS 20 HOURS BEHIND SCHEDULE.

HOLD ON TO YOUR HATS. THE WIND IS UP AND MY SLEDGE CAN CLIP ALONG AT 40 MILES PER HOUR!

WE'LL BE ALL RIGHT IF WE CAN CATCH THE NEXT TRAIN TO NEW YORK, THEN EMBARK ON THE CHINA ON DEC. 11 FROM NEW YORK TO LIVERPOOL.

ALTHOUGH THEY CAUGHT THE TRAIN TO NEW YORK, IT PULLED UP AT THE STEAMSHIP PIER AT 11:15 P.M., DEC. 11. THE CHINA HAD SAILED 35 MINUTES BEFORE.

IF ONLY I HADN'T BEEN CAPTURED! I COST MR. FOGG COUNTLESS HOURS.

PASSEPARTOUT, TAKE EVERYONE TO THE NEAREST CAFÉ AND WAIT FOR ME. BE READY TO LEAVE AT A MOMENT'S NOTICE.

AN HOUR LATER, FOGG FOUND THE HENRIETTA, A TRADING VESSEL LEAVING THAT VERY NIGHT. ITS OWNER WAS CAPTAIN ANDREW SPEEDY.

TAKE US TO LIVERPOOL, CAPTAIN. I WILL REWARD YOU HANDSOMELY.

I SAID WE ARE GOING TO BORDEAUX AND THAT'S THAT.

WILL YOU TAKE US TO BORDEAUX THEN, IF I PAY YOU $2,000 PASSAGE APIECE?

WE SAIL IN 45 MINUTES. GET YOUR PARTY ABOARD.

THE NEXT MORNING, FOGG TOOK THE BRIDGE OF THE HENRIETTA. HE HAD LOCKED CAPTAIN SPEEDY IN HIS CABIN AND PAID THE SAILORS TO HELP HIM GET TO ENGLAND.

SCOUNDREL! LET ME OUT! HOW DARE YOU TAKE MY SHIP!

MEN, FULL STEAM AHEAD! STOKE THE FIRES UNTIL THE COAL IS EXHAUSTED!

AYE-AYE, CAPTAIN FOGG.

FOGG MUST HAVE BEEN A SAILOR ONCE! LIVERPOOL, MY FOOT! I BET HE'S GOING TO SAIL SOMEWHERE HE'LL NEVER BE FOUND!

ON DEC. 18, THE ENGINEER SAID THEIR COAL WAS NEARLY USED UP. FOGG BROUGHT CAPTAIN SPEEDY ONTO THE DECK.

TO GET TO LIVERPOOL I HAVE TO BURN THE TOP HALF OF YOUR SHIP FOR FUEL. LET ME BUY YOUR SHIP FOR $60,000.

WHY, IT'S ONLY WORTH HALF THAT! I'LL TAKE IT!

BY DEC. 20, ALL THE WOOD WAS BURNED, AND THE SHIP WAS NEARLY OUT OF STEAM. FOGG HAD ONLY 24 HOURS TO REACH LONDON. JUST THEN, QUEENSLAND, IRELAND, CAME INTO SIGHT.

IF WE CAN CATCH AN EXPRESS MAIL TRAIN FROM QUEENSLAND TO DUBLIN, THEN A FAST MAIL BOAT TO LIVERPOOL, AND FINALLY A TRAIN TO LONDON, I CAN GAIN 12 HOURS.

IT'S WORTH A TRY.

FOGG DISEMBARKED ON THE LIVERPOOL PIER JUST BEFORE NOON, DEC. 21. HE WAS ONLY SIX HOURS FROM LONDON.

I ARREST YOU, PHILEAS FOGG, FOR ROBBERY, IN THE QUEEN'S NAME.

THERE MUST BE SOME MISTAKE!

FIX, YOU SCOUNDREL! HE'S INNOCENT! LET HIM GO!

TWO HOURS LATER, FIX WAS SINGING A DIFFERENT TUNE.

SIR, FORGIVE ME, A MOST UNFORTUNATE RESEMBLANCE. THE ROBBER WAS ARRESTED THREE DAYS AGO. YOU ARE FREE!

WE'VE MISSED THE EXPRESS. I'LL ORDER A SPECIAL TRAIN. LET'S GO!

BUT WHEN FOGG STEPPED FROM THE TRAIN IN LONDON, THE CLOCK READ 8:50 P.M. HE HAD LOST THE WAGER BY FIVE MINUTES.

AOUDA, THIS TRIP HAS RUINED ME. MY WEALTH IS GONE. BUT WHAT I HAVE LEFT IS YOURS TO GET YOU STARTED IN YOUR NEW LIFE.

THERE IS AN OLD SAYING THAT "MISERY ITSELF, SHARED BY TWO SYMPATHETIC SOULS, MAY BE BORNE WITH PATIENCE." WILL YOU TAKE ME FOR A KINSWOMAN AND FRIEND? WILL YOU HAVE ME FOR YOUR WIFE?

BY ALL THAT IS HOLIEST, I LOVE YOU, AOUDA! I AM ENTIRELY YOURS!

I'M SO HAPPY FOR YOU BOTH. LET'S GO HOME. I WILL TALK TO THE PREACHER AFTER CHURCH TOMORROW AND SEE IF HE CAN PERFORM THE MARRIAGE FIRST THING MONDAY.

THE NEXT EVENING, AOUDA AND FOGG WERE ENJOYING A QUIET DINNER WHEN PASSEPARTOUT BURST IN AT 8:40 P.M., BREATHLESS FROM RUNNING ALL THE WAY BACK FROM THE CHURCH.

IT'S NOT SUNDAY. IT'S SATURDAY, DEC. 21! WE GAINED A DAY BECAUSE WE TRAVELED EAST AROUND THE GLOBE. YOU MUST GET TO THE REFORM CLUB IN FIVE MINUTES!

GOOD GRIEF! I DID NOT FIGURE THAT INTO MY CALCULATIONS. OF COURSE! IF WE'D GONE WEST, WE'D HAVE LOST A DAY, BUT EAST, WE GAINED A WHOLE DAY!

FIVE SECONDS BEFORE THE CLOCK STRUCK 8:45 P.M., THE REFORM CLUB DOORS BURST OPEN.

HERE I AM, GENTLEMEN!

THREE CHEERS FOR PHILEAS FOGG!

HE CIRCLED THE GLOBE IN 80 DAYS!

FOGG AND AOUDA WERE MARRIED 48 HOURS LATER. PASSEPARTOUT GAVE THE BRIDE AWAY.

I PRONOUNCE YOU HUSBAND AND WIFE. YOU MAY NOW KISS THE BRIDE.

THE END

JULES VERNE 1828-1905

The author's life was as adventurous as that of some of his fictional characters. Like Passepartout, Verne was born in France and joined a theater troupe in Paris. Like Fogg, he was an expert sailor and an avid reader.

Verne studied topics from geology, astronomy and engineering to the latest scientific discoveries. His research allowed him to write authoritatively about fantastic subjects. Among his books were "Five Weeks in a Balloon" (1863), "Journey to the Center of the Earth" (1864), "From the Earth to the Moon" (1865), and "20,000 Leagues Under the Sea" (1870). His greatest success came with "Around the World in 80 Days," published in 1874.

In 1876, Verne bought a steam yacht he sailed throughout the world from port to port for the rest of his life. His books have been translated into many languages, adapted into plays, and made into movies and TV shows.

JULES VERNE

JULES GABRIEL VERNE WAS A PIONEER IN SCIENCE FICTION WRITING AND WROTE ABOUT TRAVELING IN SHIPS UNDERWATER AND INTO SPACE LONG BEFORE EITHER TYPE OF TRAVEL WAS POSSIBLE. VERNE WAS BORN ON FEBRUARY 8, 1828, IN NANTES, FRANCE. NANTES WAS A PORT CITY, AND VERNE LOVED THE SEA AS A BOY. HIS FATHER WAS A LAWYER, AND SENT VERNE TO PARIS TO STUDY LAW. WHILE IN PARIS, VERNE BECAME INTERESTED IN THE THEATER AND BEGAN WRITING PLAYS. HIS FATHER, HOWEVER, WAS NOT HAPPY THAT VERNE GAVE UP HIS LAW STUDIES, AND HE STOPPED SENDING VERNE MONEY. VERNE WAS FORCED TO WORK AS A STOCKBROKER, BUT HE STILL CONTINUED TO WRITE SHORT STORIES AND PLAYS. HE SPENT MUCH TIME IN THE LIBRARY, STUDYING GEOLOGY, ASTRONOMY, AND OTHER SCIENCES TO HELP HIS WRITING. IN 1863, HE PUBLISHED **FIVE WEEKS IN A BALLOON**, THE FIRST TALE IN HIS SERIES **EXTRAORDINARY JOURNEYS**. OTHER STORIES OF ADVENTURES FOLLOWED, INCLUDING **JOURNEY TO THE CENTER OF THE EARTH** (1865) AND **FROM THE EARTH TO THE MOON** (1866). HE PUBLISHED **20,000 LEAGUES UNDER THE SEA** IN 1870 AND **AROUND THE WORLD IN 80 DAYS** IN 1873. UP UNTIL HIS DEATH, HE WROTE ONE TO TWO ADVENTURE WORKS A YEAR. HE SOON BECAME WEALTHY, NOT ONLY FROM HIS NOVELS, BUT FROM PLAY PRODUCTIONS OF HIS WORK. VERNE MARRIED HONORINE DE VIANE MOREL IN 1857. THE COUPLE HAD ONE SON TOGETHER. VERNE DIED ON MARCH 24, 1905.

The Prisoner of ZENDA

A Bank Street Classic Tale

BY ANTHONY HOPE
ADAPTED BY HENRY BARKER AND E.A.M. JAKAB
ILLUSTRATIONS BY DAN SPIEGLE

I HEAR YOU AND YOUR ROYAL COUSIN RUDOLF HAVE MORE IN COMMON THAN YOUR RED HAIR AND YOUR FIRST NAMES. RUDOLF ELPHBERG SPENDS MOST OF HIS TIME IDLY, WITH NO PURPOSE IN LIFE, JUST LIKE YOU DO, RUDOLF RASSENDYLL!

COME, COME, ROSE. OUR RUDOLF HERE MAY HAVE THE RED HAIR OF OUR RURITANIAN ELPHBERG COUSINS, BUT HE'S AN ENGLISHMAN THROUGH AND THROUGH!

IN THE 19TH-CENTURY ENGLISH DINING ROOM OF MY BROTHER, LORD BURLESDON, AND HIS WIFE, ROSE, I ONCE AGAIN REALIZED I LOOKED NOTHING LIKE MY IMMEDIATE FAMILY, WITH THEIR DARK HAIR AND BLUE EYES. I FAVORED OUR HIGH-BRED COUSIN, RED-HEADED RUDOLF ELPHBERG, WHO WOULD BECOME KING OF THE TINY COUNTRY OF RURITANIA IN A VERY SHORT TIME. WHO COULD HAVE GUESSED THEN THAT MY LOOKS ALONE WOULD PLUNGE ME INTO A HARROWING ADVENTURE I WOULD NOT SOON FORGET?

RUDOLF ELPHBERG WILL BE CROWNED KING OF RURITANIA IN TWO WEEKS — RUDOLF THE FIFTH! THAT'S BOUND TO GIVE HIS LIFE SOME PURPOSE.

THE CORONATION SHOULD BE AN ENTERTAINING SPECTACLE... AND I'VE NEVER BEEN TO RURITANIA...

THERE WAS SOME TRUTH IN ROSE'S ACCUSATION. I'D SPENT MY 29 YEARS AIMLESSLY. NOW I WAS SEIZED WITH A DESIRE TO VISIT RURITANIA. I VISITED A FRIEND IN PARIS OVERNIGHT, AND THEN...

WITH THE EXCEPTION OF BERTRAND, MY FRIEND IN PARIS, NO ONE KNEW WHERE I HAD GONE. I WANTED TO KEEP IT THAT WAY.

THAT'S THE WOMAN BERTRAND POINTED OUT TO ME AT THE PARIS STATION, ANTOINETTE DE MAUBAN. SHE'S A FRIEND OF RUDOLF'S HALF-BROTHER, DUKE MICHAEL. PERHAPS SHE'S HERE FOR THE CORONATION TOO.

AT THE TOWN INN, I LEARNED STARTLING NEWS. RUDOLF'S CORONATION WOULD TAKE PLACE THE DAY AFTER TOMORROW!

THE CORONATION WAS TWO WEEKS AWAY! WHAT HAPPENED?

NOBODY WILL SAY. IF YOU ASK ME, THE FUTURE KING IS AFRAID OF HIS HALF-BROTHER, DUKE MICHAEL! AND WITH GOOD REASON!

NOW, MOTHER, THERE ARE ALWAYS RUMORS ABOUT BLACK MICHAEL. SOME SAY HE WOULD STEAL THE THRONE. AND THE KING'S BETROTHED, FLAVIA.

BY ALL THE SAINTS AND MARTYRS!! IS IT--? NO! IT CAN'T BE!! I JUST LEFT HIM AT THE CASTLE!

WHAT AILS YOU, JOHANN? THIS IS AN ENGLISH GENTLEMAN, COME TO SEE THE CORONATION.

IT'S NOT THE KING. THIS ONE HAS A BEARD AND MOUSTACHE.

I BEG YOUR PARDON, SIR. DO YOU...DO YOU KNOW OUR KING?

I'VE NEVER SEEN HIM. THOUGH I HOPE TO THE DAY AFTER TOMORROW.

I HEARD THE KING WAS VISITING DUKE MICHAEL. HOPING TO GET A GLIMPSE OF MY ROYAL COUSIN, I WANDERED INTO THE FOREST.

BUT ALL I SAW WAS THE DUKE'S SUMMER CHATEAU AND, ACROSS THE MOAT, HIS OTHER DWELLING, THE MAGNIFICENT CASTLE OF ZENDA.

I GOT SLEEPY AND DECIDED TO TAKE A NAP.

TWO MEN CAME UPON ME IN THE WOODS.

INCREDIBLE!

THE LIKENESS IS UNCANNY!

COLONEL SAPT AND FRITZ VAN TARLENHEIM WERE VERY INTERESTED TO KNOW I WAS A COUSIN OF THE ELPHBERGS. THEY TOLD ME THEY SERVED THE KING. AT THAT MOMENT--

WHO IS THIS GENTLEMAN?

A DISTANT RELATION TO YOU, SIRE. FROM ENGLAND.

RUDOLF RASSENDYLL, MAJESTY. YOUR COUSIN.

COUSIN?! YOU MUST DINE WITH US TONIGHT!

AT DINNER, WE TALKED LATE INTO THE NIGHT.

YOUR MAJESTY, IT GROWS LATE.

SIRE, THE CORONATION IS TOMORROW, AND WE MUST MAKE AN EARLY START. THE CAPITAL IS AN HOUR'S RIDE.

JUST A LITTLE WHILE LONGER. JOSEF! I'M THIRSTY! BRING ME SOMETHING TO DRINK!

HIS HIGHNESS THE DUKE BADE ME GIVE YOU THIS COLD BOTTLE OF SPARKLING LEMONADE MADE WITH SPRING WATER FROM THE ALPINE MOUNTAINS.

MY THANKS TO BLACK MICHAEL! WILL YOU JOIN ME, GENTLEMEN?

WE DECLINED, SO THE KING HAD THE LEMONADE ALL TO HIMSELF. UNFORTUNATELY, THE NEXT MORNING...

WHA---?

GET UP, MAN! SOMETHING TERRIBLE HAS HAPPENED!

THE KING IS DRUGGED. LOOKS AS THOUGH HE WON'T COME TO FOR SEVERAL HOURS. AND THE CORONATION'S AT NOON!

I'LL WAGER THIS IS BLACK MICHAEL'S DOING.

HE MUST HAVE DRUGGED THE LEMONADE!

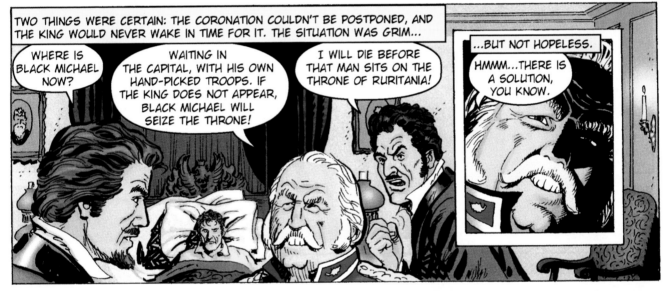

TWO THINGS WERE CERTAIN: THE CORONATION COULDN'T BE POSTPONED, AND THE KING WOULD NEVER WAKE IN TIME FOR IT. THE SITUATION WAS GRIM...

WHERE IS BLACK MICHAEL NOW?

WAITING IN THE CAPITAL, WITH HIS OWN HAND-PICKED TROOPS. IF THE KING DOES NOT APPEAR, BLACK MICHAEL WILL SEIZE THE THRONE!

I WILL DIE BEFORE THAT MAN SITS ON THE THRONE OF RURITANIA!

...BUT NOT HOPELESS.

HMMM...THERE IS A SOLUTION, YOU KNOW.

HURRIEDLY, COLONEL SAPT CONVINCED ME TO SHAVE MY BEARD AND MOUSTACHE AND TAKE THE PLACE OF MY COUSIN.

I CANNOT WAIT TO SEE BLACK MICHAEL'S FACE!

WE WILL HIDE THE KING IN THE CELLAR OF OUR HUNTING LODGE, AND COME BACK FOR HIM TONIGHT, AFTER THE CORONATION.

AS WE RODE TO THE CAPITAL FOR THE CORONATION, COLONEL SAPT BRIEFED ME ON WHAT TO DO AND THE DIGNITARIES AND RELATIVES I WOULD MEET.

WHEN PEOPLE LINE UP IN THE CATHEDRAL, YOU MUST KISS THEM, ONE BY ONE.

KISS THEM?

IT IS CUSTOMARY.

FINALLY WE ARRIVED AT STRELSAU, THE CAPITAL. HUGE CROWDS WERE EVERYWHERE.

AH, I COULD GET TO LIKE THIS.

RED ROSES FOR THE RED ELPHBERGS!

IF HE'S RED, HE'S RIGHT!!

JUDGE FOR YOURSELVES HOW RED I AM!

I KNEW ANTOINETTE DE MALIBAN AND DUKE MICHAEL WERE CLOSE. SHE MUST HAVE KNOWN THAT I WAS AN IMPOSTER! WOULD SHE TELL THE DUKE? I HOPED THE RED ROSE SHE HELD MEANT SHE WOULD NOT.

THE WOMAN FROM THE TRAIN STATION— ANTOINETTE DE MALIBAN!

THE CHOIR SANG. THE ORGAN PLAYED. MIRACULOUSLY, EVEN PRINCESS FLAVIA, THE KING'S INTENDED, DIDN'T REALIZE I WAS AN IMPOSTER! THE BISHOP PLACED THE CROWN ON MY HEAD. I WAS A KING.

ARISE, RUDOLF THE FIFTH!

MY DEAR BROTHER MICHAEL! HOW GOOD TO SEE YOU.

FLAVIA, I'M SO GLAD TO SEE YOU, MY DEAR!

SHE'S THE LOVELIEST WOMAN I'VE EVER SEEN!

YOUR MAJESTY.

I COULDN'T HELP MYSELF! BESIDES, SAPT SAID IT WAS THE CUSTOM.

WHEN'S THE WEDDING?

YOU'RE THE KING NOW! MAKE HER YOUR QUEEN!

YOU LOOK DIFFERENT, RUDOLF. THINNER. AND CALMER. HAVE YOU BEGUN TO TAKE THINGS MORE SERIOUSLY?

WOULD THAT PLEASE YOU?

BEFORE FLAVIA COULD REPLY, OUR PRECIOUS TIME ALONE TOGETHER WAS OVER. WE HAD ARRIVED AT THE PALACE...

WHY, YES.

LATER, IN THE KING'S DRESSING ROOM, I REALIZED THAT MY TIME AS KING—AND AS FLAVIA'S BETROTHED—WAS ALMOST OVER.

SHE'S SO BEAUTIFUL!

NEVER MIND HER! YOU AND COLONEL SAPT MUST START BACK TO ZENDA. THE KING SHOULD BE WAKING UP BY NOW.

COLONEL SAPT AND I RODE TO ZENDA TO FETCH THE REAL KING.

YET WE WEREN'T THE ONLY ONES RIDING TO ZENDA THAT NIGHT.

IT'S BLACK MICHAEL!

TO ZENDA, THEN!

FEARING THAT BLACK MICHAEL WAS UP TO SOME MISCHIEF, WE HURRIED TO THE HUNTING LODGE WHERE WE HAD HIDDEN THE KING.

JOSEF, THE SERVANT, HAS BEEN MURDERED!

THE KING! HE'S GONE!

BACK UPSTAIRS, COLONEL SAPT INSISTED I CONTINUE MY MASQUERADE.

WE MUST GO BACK TO THE CAPITAL AND DENOUNCE BLACK MICHAEL. HE'S KIDNAPPED THE KING!

NO, WE MUST GO BACK AS THE CROWNED KING AND HIS LOYAL SERVANT AND SAY NOTHING. WITH YOU AS KING, MICHAEL CANNOT SEIZE POWER. AND HE CANNOT EXPOSE YOU BECAUSE THEN HIS CRIME WILL BECOME KNOWN. IF YOU KEEP PLAYING THE KING, WE HAVE A CHANCE TO SAVE THE *REAL* KING.

RIDING HARD, WE REACHED STRELSAU AT DAWN.

WHEN FRITZ HEARD ABOUT THE KING'S KIDNAPPING, HE URGED COLONEL SAPT TO TAKE ACTION.

WE MUST DO SOMETHING AT ONCE!

YET WE MUST TAKE NO CHANCES.

PERHAPS YOU ARE RIGHT TO BE CAUTIOUS. I HEARD THAT HALF OF THE SIX HAVE ARRIVED IN STRELSAU--THE THREE FOREIGNERS. NO ONE KNOWS WHERE THE OTHER THREE, THE RURITANIANS, ARE.

AHA! I'LL WAGER MICHAEL HAS THE THREE RURITANIANS GUARDING THE KING IN SOME HIDEOUT. THAT'S WHY HE SENT FOR THE FOREIGNERS. HE NEEDS THEM TO GUARD HIM!

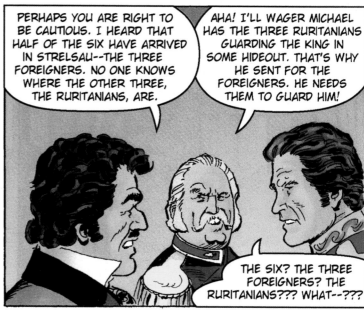

THE SIX? THE THREE FOREIGNERS? THE RURITANIANS??? WHAT--???

COLONEL SAPT TOLD ME THE SIX WERE BLACK MICHAEL'S PERSONAL BODYGUARDS, A BAND OF VICIOUS CUTTHROATS: THREE RURITANIANS AND THREE FOREIGNERS--AN ENGLISHMAN, A FRENCHMAN AND A BELGIAN.

THE SIX ARE VERY DANGEROUS, SO WE MUST BE CAREFUL. IF WE CAN FIND THE THREE RURITANIANS--HENTZAU AND HIS TWO HENCHMEN--WE'LL FIND THE KING.

WE MUST GET OUR SPY NETWORK INTO OPERATION!

HOW CAN I HELP?

PLAY THE PART OF THE KING!

AND SO I DID.

PRINCESS FLAVIA WILL LOVE THESE. THANK YOU.

YOU'RE WELCOME, MAJESTY!

WHILE FRITZ AND COLONEL SAPT CONSULTED WITH THEIR SPIES, I CALLED ON PRINCESS FLAVIA.

HOW WONDERFUL! YOU'VE NEVER BROUGHT ME FLOWERS!

I WILL BRING THEM TO YOU EVERY DAY--THAT IS, IF YOU WOULD LIKE ME TO.

HE NEVER BROUGHT HER FLOWERS?! INCREDIBLE!

OH, YES, I WOULD LIKE THAT. BUT I WOULD LIKE SOMETHING ELSE EVEN MORE. THEY SAY BLACK MICHAEL, THE DUKE, PLOTS AGAINST YOU. PLEASE BE CAREFUL.

SHE CARES!

I WILL.

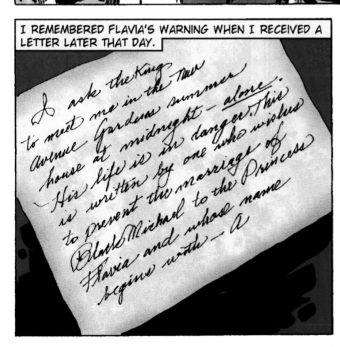

I REMEMBERED FLAVIA'S WARNING WHEN I RECEIVED A LETTER LATER THAT DAY.

I ask the King to meet me in the New Avenue Gardens house at midnight --alone-- His life is in danger. This is written by one who wishes to prevent the marriage of Black Michael to the Princess Flavia and whose name begins with --A

ANTOINETTE DE MAUBAN! SHE COULD HELP US FIND THE KING--IF SHE CHOSE.

47

DESPITE THE DANGER, I DECIDED TO MEET WITH MADAME DE MAUBAN.

MR. RASSENDYLL! THE DUKE ORDERED ME TO WRITE THAT NOTE. THREE MEN-- THREE OF THE SIX--ARE COMING HERE TO KILL YOU. YOU MUST LEAVE!

AND THE KING? WHERE IS HE?

SUDDENLY WE HEARD FOOTSTEPS.

THE ASSASSINS ARE HERE ALREADY!

ANTOINETTE WHISPERED TO ME THE LOCATION OF THE KING AND TOLD ME THE THREE MEN OUTSIDE WERE THE FOREIGNERS.

MR. RASSENDYLL, COME OUTSIDE! I CAN OFFER YOU SAFE CONDUCT TO THE BORDER AND MONEY.

GIVE ME A MOMENT TO CONSIDER.

DON'T TRUST THEM!

I HAD ONLY ONE HOPE OF ESCAPE. I WHISPERED TO ANTOINETTE TO STAND CLOSE TO THE WALL, OUT OF THE LINE OF FIRE.

GENTLEMEN, I ACCEPT YOUR OFFER. DO COME IN SO WE CAN SHAKE ON IT.

THE SECOND THE DOOR OPENED, I SPRANG INTO ACTION.

I GOT AWAY WITHOUT A SCRATCH!

GOOD WORK! NOW THAT WE KNOW WHERE THE KING IS, WE CAN PLAN HIS RESCUE.

BUT WE MUST ACT AS IF EVERYTHING IS NORMAL. TOMORROW NIGHT WE MUST ALL ATTEND A BALL IN HONOR OF PRINCESS FLAVIA. THE PEOPLE ARE EAGER FOR A ROYAL WEDDING, YOU KNOW.

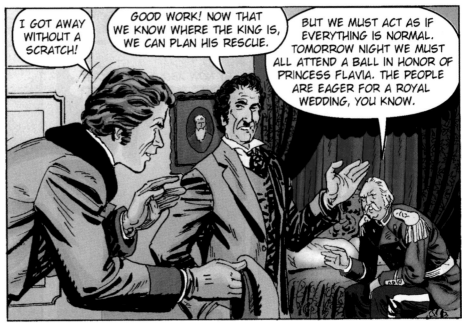

COLONEL SAPT URGED ME TO PROPOSE TO FLAVIA. WHEN I SAID I DIDN'T WANT TO LIE TO HER, HE SAID I WAS LYING ALREADY. I REALIZED HE WOULD DO ANYTHING TO KEEP BLACK MICHAEL FROM THE THRONE, EVEN TO KEEPING AN IMPOSTER THERE.

WHEN WE WERE ALONE, I LEARNED THAT FLAVIA LOVED ME--RUPERT RASSENDYLL--AND NOT THE REAL KING.

I LOVE YOU, RUDOLF. I NEVER DID BEFORE-- WELL, BEFORE THE CORONATION. BUT I DO NOW, WITH ALL MY HEART.

I--I LOVE YOU TOO, FLAVIA.

AT THAT MOMENT THE TEMPTATION TO END THIS MASQUERADE NEARLY OVERCAME ME...BUT COLONEL SAPT INTERVENED.

FLAVIA, I--I MUST TELL YOU SOMETHING! I'M NOT THE--

A-HEM. EXCUSE ME, SIRE. THE CARDINAL WISHES TO BID YOU FAREWELL.

BY THE TIME WE LEFT THE BALL, THE COLONEL HAD TOLD ALL OF STRELSAU THAT FLAVIA AND I SOON WOULD BE MARRIED.

LATER, TERRIBLE THOUGHTS ASSAILED ME. I FELT AS IF THE DEVIL HIMSELF WERE TEMPTING ME.

WHAT IF I DID NOTHING, AND BLACK MICHAEL KILLED THE KING? THEN I COULD KILL MICHAEL AND MARRY FLAVIA! NO ONE WOULD KNOW EXCEPT FRITZ AND COLONEL SAPT. AND SAPT WOULDN'T CARE AS LONG AS MICHAEL WAS DEAD.

TO SAVE MY HONOR--AND TO SAVE MY VERY SOUL--I HAD TO SAVE THE KING!

WHERE ARE YOU GOING?

TO ZENDA, TO SAVE THE KING.

I'M COMING WITH YOU!

COLONEL SAPT CONVINCED ME TO WAIT UNTIL MORNING AND TO CALL OUR EXPEDITION A HUNTING TRIP. WE RODE TO FRITZ'S CASTLE, A FEW MILES FROM THE CASTLE AT ZENDA, WHERE THE KING WAS HELD.

BLACK MICHAEL MUST KNOW BY NOW ABOUT THIS "BOAR HUNT." AND I DON'T THINK HE WILL BE FOOLED.

AS SOON AS WE ARRIVED, WE HAD VISITORS, THE THREE RURITANIAN MEMBERS OF THE SIX: LAUENGRAM, KRAFSTEIN, AND THEIR LEADER, HENTZAU.

THE DUKE WELCOMES YOU TO ZENDA, SIRE. HE WOULD ASK YOU TO STAY WITH HIM, BUT HE IS ILL WITH SCARLET FEVER--A MOST INFECTIOUS DISEASE. MOST INFECTIOUS.

I WOULD NOT LIKE TO BE... INFECTED. PLEASE ASSURE THE DUKE THAT I WILL STAY FAR FROM THE CASTLE.

UNTIL TONIGHT!

LATER THAT DAY, I MET WITH JOHANN, THE KEEPER OF BLACK MICHAEL'S CASTLE. FOR A BAG OF GOLD, HE TOLD ME THE LOCATION OF THE KING'S CELL AND HIS GUARDS' SCHEDULE. AND ALSO THAT THE KING HAD TAKEN ILL AND WAS BEING NURSED BY ANTOINETTE DE MAUBAN. AND MORE...

THAT VILLAIN HENZAU IS ENAMORED OF MADAME DE MAUBAN. BLACK MICHAEL IS FURIOUS. THE TWO MEN ARE ALMOST READY TO CROSS SWORDS OVER HER!

IT WAS TIME TO RECONNOITER THE CASTLE OF ZENDA SO WE COULD MAKE OUR RESCUE PLANS.

I SWAM THE MOAT TO THE CASTLE OF ZENDA.

I HEARD VOICES--A PIPE LED INTO THE KING'S CELL. I COULD HEAR DETCHARD, ONE OF THE FOREIGNERS, TALKING TO THE KING.

TIME FOR YOUR CHAINS.

WHY DOESN'T BLACK MICHAEL JUST KILL ME AND BE DONE WITH IT? I AM DYING BY INCHES!

YOUR HALF-BROTHER DOES NOT WISH YOU DEAD YET.

--MORE CLEARLY THAN WORDS, THE WEAKNESS IN THE KING'S VOICE TOLD ME THAT TIME WAS RUNNING OUT...AND ONCE THE KING WAS DEAD, HIS BODY COULD BE PUSHED THROUGH THE PIPE INTO THE MOAT, WHERE IT WOULD DISAPPEAR FOREVER. WE HAD TO WORK FAST!

THE NEXT DAY, AS WE HURRIEDLY MADE OUR PLANS, WE ENCOUNTERED A NEW PROBLEM IN THE PERSON OF STRELSAU'S CHIEF OF POLICE.

WHY, CHIEF! WHAT BRINGS YOU TO ZENDA?

YOUR MAJESTY, THE BRITISH AMBASSADOR REPORTS THAT A YOUNG COUNTRYMAN OF HIS NAMED RUDOLF RASSENDYLL IS MISSING. HE WAS LAST SEEN IN ZENDA.

I HAD TO THROW THE CHIEF OFF MY TRAIL!

IT IS BELIEVED HE WAS FOLLOWING A CERTAIN MADAME DE MAUBAN. THE AMBASSADOR FEARS FOUL PLAY.

I HAVE HEARD HER NAME IN CONNECTION WITH BLACK MICHAEL. CHIEF, WE MUST AVOID A SCANDAL AT ALL COSTS! PLEASE RETURN TO STRELSAU. I WILL SEE TO THIS MATTER MYSELF.

WITH MY FAMILY NOW SEARCHING FOR ME, AND THE KING IN BAD HEALTH, IT BECAME URGENT TO RESCUE HIM QUICKLY. MY PLAN WOULD ONLY WORK WITH SPLIT-SECOND TIMING, JOHANN'S HELP--AND LUCK.

THE PRISONER IS VERY ILL, SIRE. THE DUKE HAS SUMMONED A PHYSICIAN.

YOU HAVE YOUR BAG OF GOLD. OPEN THE CASTLE DOOR AT 2 A.M. TONIGHT. NOT A MOMENT LATER!

YES, SIRE!

ONE OF THE RURITANIANS--HENTZAU--UPSET OUR CAREFULLY LAID PLANS WHEN HE PRESSED HIS ATTENTIONS ON ANTOINETTE. HER TERRIFIED SCREAMS BROUGHT BLACK MICHAEL TO HER RESCUE. THE TWO MEN BEGAN A FIGHT TO THE DEATH.

GET OUT, AND LEAVE ANTOINETTE ALONE!

THIS DOG NO LONGER OBEYS ITS MASTER!

STOP! PLEASE! I BEG YOU!

IT WAS TIME FOR ME TO ENTER THE CASTLE DOOR JOHANN HAD LEFT OPEN.

BONG! BONG!

AS I WAS ABOUT TO GO IN THE CASTLE DOOR, DE GAUTET RAN OUT.

WHO IS--? AAARGH!

RUNNING DOWN TO THE KING'S CELL, I MET BERSONIN RUNNING UP.

YOU? AAARGH!

I RUSHED INTO THE KING'S CELL JUST IN THE NICK OF TIME. DETCHARD HAD KILLED THE ATTENDING DOCTOR AND WAS ABOUT TO MURDER THE KING.

STOP, MURDERER!

PREPARE TO DIE, IMPOSTER!

DETCHARD WAS A FAR BETTER SWORDSMAN THAN I WAS. DEATH, IT SEEMED, WAS IN STORE FOR BOTH RUDOLFS. AND THEN--

COUSIN RUDOLF! I'LL HELP YOU!

OOF!

DETCHARD WAS OUT OF COMMISSION. BUT THE KING AND I WERE NOT YET SAFE.

WHILE THAT VILLAIN HENTZAU WAS AT LARGE, NO ONE WAS SAFE.

FIGHT, YOU COWARDS!

BLACK MICHAEL IS DEAD! YOU MONSTER! YOU'VE KILLED THE MAN I LOVE.

GOOD! DROP YOUR WEAPONS, ALL OF YOU! I'M YOUR MASTER NOW!

NEVER!

BANG

HAH! YOU MISSED!

HE'S GETTING AWAY!

NOT IF I CAN HELP IT!

COLONEL SAPT AND FRITZ WOULD WHISK THE KING TO SAFETY. I WOULD BRING HENTZAU TO JUSTICE--OR DIE TRYING.

BUT HENTZAU SEEMED TO HAVE PLANNED EVERYTHING PERFECTLY-- EVEN HIS ESCAPE!

FAREWELL, RUDOLF RASSENDYLL!

COME BACK HERE AND FIGHT, YOU DEVIL!

BE GRATEFUL I WILL NOT!

AND THEN HE VANISHED--VILE AND UNCONQUERED. MY DISAPPOINTMENT WAS TEMPERED ONLY BY THE KNOWLEDGE THAT THE KING WAS SAFE AT LAST.

EXHAUSTED FROM THE KING'S RESCUE AND MY PURSUIT OF HENTZAU, I RESTED FOR A MOMENT IN THE KING'S EMPTY CELL. BUT SUDDENLY--

RUDOLF, MY DARLING! ARE YOU HURT?

FLAVIA! DEAREST! I--I...

MADAME-- HE IS NOT THE KING!

MY MASQUERADE WAS AT AN END. I HAD SAVED THE KING BUT LOST THE WOMAN I LOVED.

WHAT DO YOU MEAN?

AT FIRST FLAVIA REFUSED TO BELIEVE I WAS NOT THE KING. FINALLY SHE ACCEPTED THE TRUTH. THE NEXT DAY, WE SAID OUR PAINFUL FAREWELLS.

I WILL ALWAYS LOVE YOU, RUDOLF.

AND I WILL ALWAYS LOVE YOU--WITH ALL MY HEART. BUT--

I KNOW, MY DARLING...

FLAVIA REMAINED WHERE SHE BELONGED-- IN RURITANIA, WITH HER PEOPLE, AND HER KING. I LEFT THAT VERY NIGHT.

WE FOUGHT THE GOOD FIGHT, DIDN'T WE, COLONEL?

WE DEFEATED THOSE TRAITORS AND SET THE KING FIRMLY ON THE THRONE.

HEAVEN DOESN'T ALWAYS MAKE THE RIGHT MEN KINGS!

AND SO WE THREE BID A FINAL FAREWELL.

THE FOLLOWING EVENING IN LONDON, I HAD A LOT OF EXPLAINING TO DO--WHICH I DIDN'T DO.

RUDOLF, YOU MUST LET US KNOW WHERE YOU ARE THE NEXT TIME YOU TRAVEL. WE WERE WORRIED! WE THOUGHT YOU'D BEEN KIDNAPPED! WHATEVER WERE YOU DOING?

NOW, NOW, DEAR. RUDOLF IS FREE TO GO WHEREVER HE PLEASES.

LET'S JUST SAY I WASN'T MYSELF FOR A WHILE.

I WENT ON TO HAVE A FULL AND PRODUCTIVE LIFE. BUT FLAVIA ALWAYS REMAINED MY ONE TRUE LOVE. AND, AS IT TURNED OUT, I REMAINED HERS.

PLEASE...PLEASE THANK THE QUEEN FOR ME.

AS ALWAYS, MY FRIEND.

Rudolf - Flavia forever

THE END

ANTHONY HOPE

ANTHONY HOPE WAS BORN ANTHONY HOPE HAWKINS ON FEBRUARY 9, 1863, IN LONDON, ENGLAND. HIS FATHER WAS A CLERGYMAN AND PRINCIPAL OF A GRADE SCHOOL, WHICH HOPE ATTENDED. HOPE LATER WENT TO COLLEGE, WHERE HE EDITED HIS SCHOOL NEWSPAPER. HE STUDIED LAW AND BEGAN A CAREER IN LAW IN 1887. IN HIS FREE TIME, HE BEGAN WRITING, AND HE PUBLISHED HIS FIRST NOVEL, **A MAN OF MARK**, IN 1890. AFTER PUBLISHING HIS THIRD NOVEL, **MR. WITT'S WIDOW** (1892), AND HIS FOURTH NOVEL, **THE PRISONER OF ZENDA** (1894), HE BECAME SUCCESSFUL ENOUGH AS A WRITER TO GIVE UP HIS LAW CAREER. **THE PRISONER OF ZENDA** IS SET IN THE FICTIONAL GERMAN KINGDOM OF RURITANIA, THE NOVEL WAS SO POPULAR THAT IT WAS TURNED INTO A PLAY FOR THEATER PRODUCTIONS. HOPE CONTINUED TO WRITE NOVELS, INCLUDING **RUPERT OF HENTZAU** (1898), A SEQUEL TO **THE PRISONER OF ZENDA**. DURING WORLD WAR I, HE WORKED FOR GREAT BRITAIN'S MINISTRY OF INFORMATION AND HELPED WRITE WAR PROPAGANDA. HE WAS KNIGHTED BY THE BRITISH KING IN 1918 FOR HIS SERVICES. HE AND HIS WIFE ELIZABETH SOMERVILLE HAWKINS HAD THREE CHILDREN TOGETHER. HOPE DIED OF CANCER IN 1933. **THE PRISONER OF ZENDA** HAS SINCE BEEN ADAPTED FOR TELEVISION AND MOVIE PRODUCTIONS. THE MOST POPULAR MOVIE VERSION WAS MADE IN 1937.